MAKING WELSH LOVE SPOONS
AND
OTHER SMALL CARVINGS

J. ELGER

ISBN 1-903314-52-6

Printed by Gwasg Pantycelyn, Caernarfon

INTRODUCTION

I have written this booklet to encourage people to take up woodcarving as a hobby, not a hobby from which you will make much money, but at least one which will in quite a short time pay for itself if you wish it to.

We sometimes start a hobby early in life and continue our interest throughout our lifetime. My father was a Cornish sea fisherman and from an early age he took me fishing. My love of sea fishing has continued until the present day, when I am now over 80 years old.

Approaching retirement age I began to think that I needed another hobby which I could enjoy when the weather was uninviting for walking or fishing. I had always been interested in making things and looking at things that other people had made and this led me to the gentle art of woodcarving. It is now about 20 years since I started and during this time it has brought a great deal of pleasure to both my wife and myself.

After several years carving I joined the Anglesey Craftworkers Guild and have since taken part in many Craft Fairs held on the Island.

The fact that I will never become an expert woodcarver is not important, there has obviously been an improvement from the time when I first started, more importantly it gives me an aim in life, something to get up for in the morning, something which you would willingly miss a meal for if you are busy in a creative part of the process.

Some of our best wood carvers are ladies, very little physical strength is required, you choose the type of work you think you are capable of at any stage of your development and enjoy it. I started by carving Welsh Love Spoons, these can be very simple in design or very complex, the choice is yours. I would like to dedicate this booklet to my dear wife Ivy, without whose help and encouragement it would never have been produced. I also have to thank her for her contribution in the workshop. If as sometimes happens, I become snowed under with work, she will mark out, drill, fretsaw, bandsaw and varnish our output, leaving me to do the more intricate work. She has also been invaluable helping to set-up and man the stall at craft fairs. If you should decide to take up woodcarving I hope it will be as rewarding for you as it has been for us.

WELSH LOVE SPOONS

Wood is clean and warm to work with unlike metals which are cold and dirty. Metals need expensive machines for model making whereas small wooden items can be made with a very modest collection of hand tools most of which may already be available in your own home D.I.Y. kit. Having decided to work with wood, the next step was to choose what to make. My experience of carpentry was practically nil, so it had to be something simple.

Having lived and worked in Wales for a number of years I was familiar with Welsh Love Spoons which were to be seen in most gift shops. Many of these spoons are mass produced and are of indifferent quality, but there are some really fine examples to be found if you look for them, these are usually produced in small numbers by individual craftsmen.

One of the best places to see a collection of spoons made by modern craftsmen is in The Lovespoon Shop, opposite Cardiff castle.

There are a number of advantages in choosing to make love spoons, they can be simple or complicated so that as your skill increases, so too can the complexity of the design. As the amount of wood required for each spoon is small, the cost of materials is very low. Finally if a breakage should occur, very little has been lost except your own time and effort.

The spoons I make are all made from hardwood, it is easier to work with and easier to obtain a good finish on the final product. After using a variety of woods you will soon find which you prefer, personally I like mahogany, but this is becoming increasingly difficult to obtain from timber suppliers.

A useful source of supply is old damaged furniture which can often be bought at auction sales quite cheaply, friends and neighbours have also provided me with some very useful pieces of timber.

There is no written history about Welsh Love Spoons as these were first made more than three hundred years ago by farm labourers, seamen and other manual workers who for the most part were unable to either read or write. Domestic spoons at that time were invariably made from wood, often sycamore, as metal spoons were made from bronze, silver or in some cases gold, all of which were expensive and beyond the means of most working people.

We know the age of some spoons because a number of examples are to be seen in St. Fagans Museum, near Cardiff, which have dates carved on them. It is thought that spoons were often given as an indication of the affection of the spoonmaker for a certain young lady, in much the same way as a bunch of flowers, a box of chocolates or a piece of jewellery might be given today.

The following list gives some of the symbols to be found on love spoons today:

Heart	–	love or affection
Wheel	–	I will work for you
Bell	–	marriage
Anchor	–	steadfast love
Double bowl	–	togetherness
Horseshoe	–	good luck
Key or keyhole	–	my home is yours
Padlock	–	security
Knot	–	eternal love
Twisted stem	–	two lives become as one
Balls in cage	–	love held safe
Chain links	–	linking together the lives of two people

The last two symbols are often said to be an indication of the number of children hoped for in a marriage, more probably they were used to show the dexterity and patience of one wood carver compared with another spoonmaker.

Tools required

It is desirable but not essential to have a bench fitted with either a metal or woodworkers vice. An electric drill together with a drill stand. A variety of twist drills. A coping saw, tenon saw and a keyhole saw. One or two gouges, 12mm. and 25mm. would be useful to start with. A mallet (I find the cylindrical variety preferable to the flat faced mallet). A variety of files, round, half round and flat. Bastard cut are better than fine cut for most woodworking applications. Stanley knives or other fixed blade knives. Various grades of sand paper. In addition to the tools listed above, I have over the years acquired an electric fretsaw, a belt sander, and a band saw. There are two basic designs of band saw, the two wheel and the three wheel, the three wheel variety is generally smaller and cheaper but the blades, due to the smaller working radius, invariably seem to have a shorter working life.

Design

There are no rules that have to be followed in your design but invariably one or more hearts will be incorporated. Some typical spoons that I have made and some made by other carvers are shown on adjacent pages.

Most of the early spoons that I made varied in length from 20-30cm. by 5cm. wide by lcm. thick. Having selected a suitable piece of wood, the chosen design should be drawn out on the flat face. If your drawing is good this may be done freehand but for most people it would be better to use a ruler and compasses. A suitable sized domestic spoon can be used as a template for the bowl. A useful additional piece of equipment for marking out, are the plastic templates available from stationers which have circles and ellipses of varying sizes.

I find it best to hollow out the bowl first whilst the wood is still easy to hold in the vice. To do this I use two gouges of different sizes Fig. 1. Holding the smaller gouge at the corner of the spoon at an angle of about 60 degrees, give one or two sharp blows with the mallet, the flatter gouge can now be used to link up the two previous cuts. The small gouge is now taken to the front edge of the spoon and successive cuts are made to produce the bowl to the required depth. The bowl can be smoothed to a good shape using a spherical Carborundum stone held in the drilling machine, the final hand sanding can be left until the spoon is completed.

Having completed the bowl, the sequence of subsequent operations is less important. I usually drill holes of the appropriate size wherever they are required. The profile can then be cut out using a coping saw, fret saw or band saw if available. Any internal shapes can be fashioned using a coping saw or fretsaw. The surplus wood on the back of the spoon can be removed using a knife. The profile, openings and the back of the spoon can be finished using appropriate files.

Using various grades of sandpaper the desired finish can be obtained before varnishing or polishing. I normally use satin finish polyurethane varnish for most of my work. Two or three coats are usually required, rubbing down lightly with a fine sandpaper between coats.

One of the great attractions of making love spoons is that no two designs need to be alike.

One of the most intriguing features of love spoons are the captive balls. To be authentic these must be made from the same piece of wood and are carved in situ. For a first attempt it will probably be best to practice on a scrap piece of wood. Make this 25mm. square section and about 10cm. or more long. Mark out each face carefully as shown in Fig. 2.

Drill the 12mm. holes from each side until they meet near the centre of the wood, this avoids any rough edges on the hole which sometimes results if the holes are drilled from one side

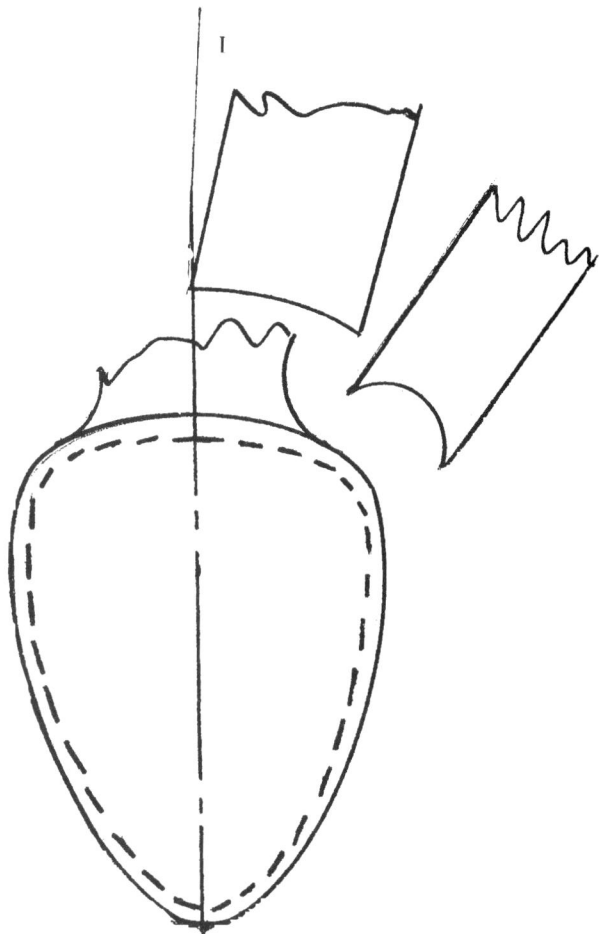

FIG. 1

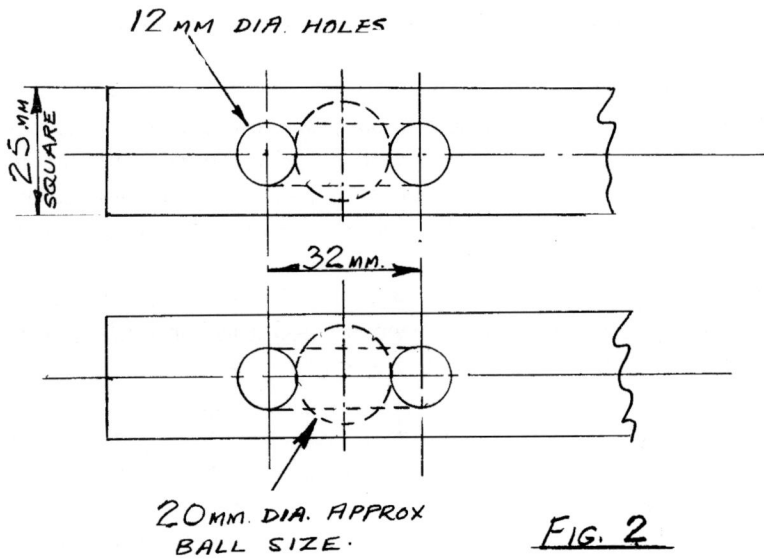

12 MM DIA. HOLES

25 MM SQUARE

32 MM.

20 MM. DIA. APPROX BALL SIZE.

FIG. 2

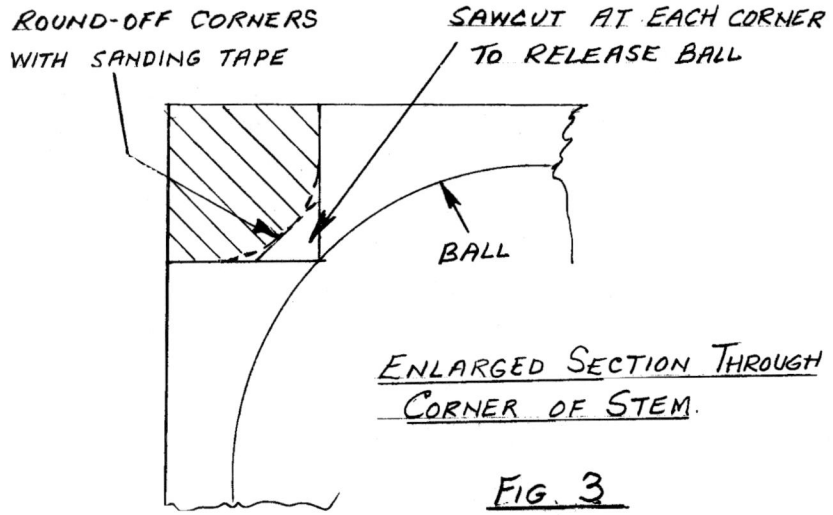

ROUND-OFF CORNERS WITH SANDING TAPE

SAWCUT AT EACH CORNER TO RELEASE BALL

BALL

ENLARGED SECTION THROUGH CORNER OF STEM.

FIG. 3

only. Accurate marking out is necessary to ensure holes lining up.

Using a knife, in my case I use a Stanley knife, you cut away surplus wood from around the ball, care must be taken at this stage not to remove too much wood or else the ball will end up too small and fall out of its cage. It helps if you can visualise the ball in its final position as you are cutting the wood away. Looking on one face of the wood, the top surface of the ball would be approximately 2.5mm. below the surface of the wood.

Part of the cage has now been formed and the knife can be used to chamfer the inside corner of the cage to meet the ball. This is shown in Fig. 3. The ball is now held at four points where it touches the cage and it can be released using a coping saw or other thin bladed saw. When the ball has been released it will be fairly rough and will not move up and down the cage freely. Some movement will be possible and a small square file can be used to smooth and round off the ball. I have ground off the cutting edges from the teeth on either side of the file to prevent the cage from being accidentally filed. Fig. 4. This rounding off may take some time at first but as the knife work improves it will soon become quicker. The inside of the cage legs can be finished using a piece of sanding tape to give a nice rounded corner allowing greater movement of the ball without increasing the size of the cage appreciably. As skill increases the size of the cage and balls can be reduced by adjusting the various dimensions.

The chain is another feature to be found with some spoons, this again should be an integral part of the spoon and made from the same length of wood. A practice run is again advisable so that you can find out if there are any snags that I have not brought to your attention. This time you will need a piece of wood 25mm. square and about 20cm. long. Mark out the wood as shown in Fig. 5 some of this marking out may be dispensed with on later work but is advisable when making your first attempt.

The sequence of operations and method of producing a chain may vary from one person to another, as with all the other

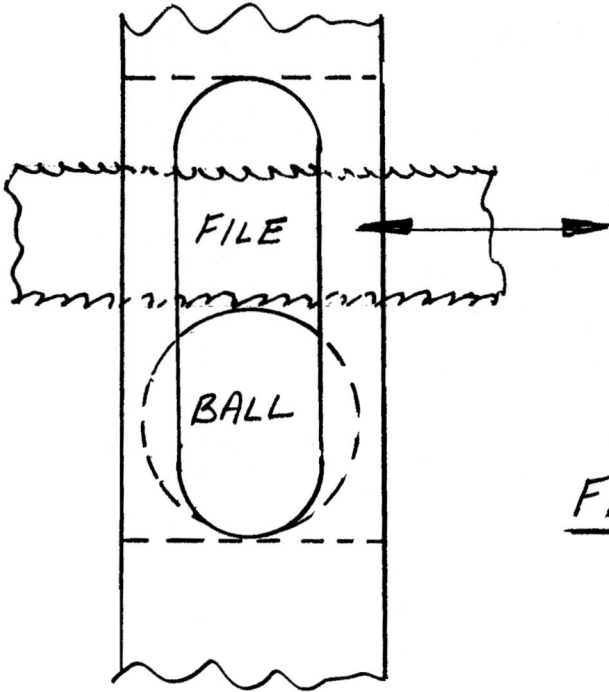

FILE

BALL

FIG. 4

25 MM SQ.

45 MM.

45 MM

6 MM

45 MM

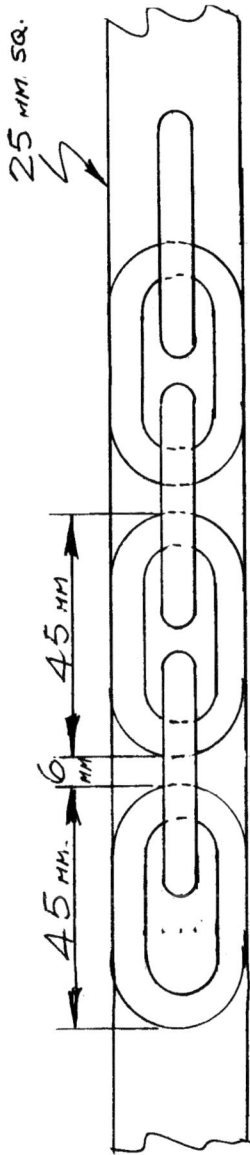

SEQUENCE OF OPERATIONS.

MARK OUT.

DRILL HOLES.

CUT AWAY SURPLUS WOOD. (SHOWN SHADED)

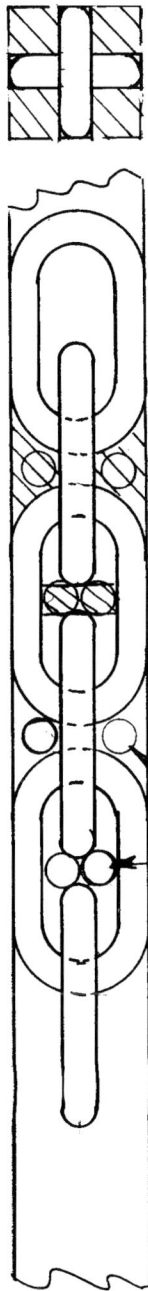

6 MM. DIA.

FIG. 5

13

methods described in this book, these are the methods that I use which suits the equipment I have available.

First drill the holes as indicated in the sketch then using a knife or saw remove most of the surplus wood from the end of each link. Finish the profile with a file. The internal holes should be linked up using a knife and cleaned up using a small square file. A tenon saw or knife can be used to remove the corners of the square leaving a cruciform section. Using a keyhole saw and starting from the drilled holes, cut along the inside of each link to a point midway between the ends of a pair of links. The links can now be separated by removing the small tongue of wood holding the links together, this is best done using a small electric hand drill and a 1.5mm. drill or burr. Fig. 6. However careful you are the links will still be in a fairly rough state and will require a considerable amount of hand work using a knife, file and sandpaper to bring them to a state of near uniformity. Don't be disappointed by your first efforts, I promise things will soon get better.

Another feature that sometimes appears on spoons is the twist or spiral, this may take the form of a surface groove or it may be cut right through the stem, the methods used to produce these grooves differs somewhat. Taking the surface groove first, you start off by producing a square section of stem where the spiral is to be formed. You can reduce this to an octagonal section by filing away the corners of the square section, the stem can easily be made cylindrical by a little more filing at each corner. If you are lucky enough to possess a lathe you can produce your cylinder on the machine leaving enough wood at each end for the bowl and whatever else you may wish to incorporate in your design at the other end.

Having made the cylinder, the path of the groove can be drawn on the stem in the following way. First measure the diameter of the cylinder as accurately as you can and multiply this by Pi (3.14). Suppose the diameter of the cylinder was 25 mm. This multiplied by 3.14 would equal 78.5 mm. say 79. We will say that the length of the groove that you wish to produce is

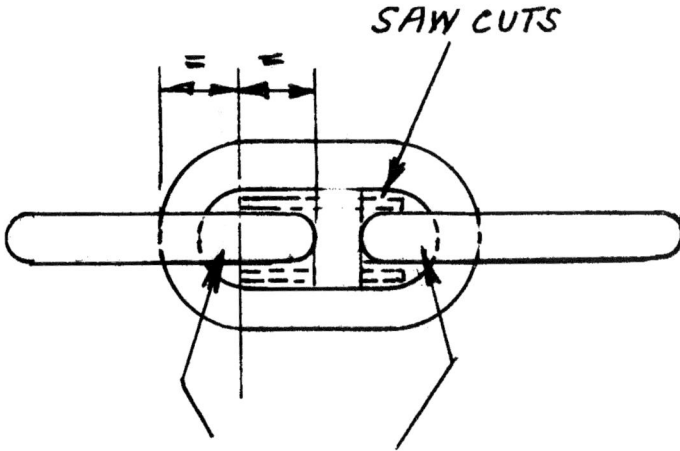

SAW CUTS

SMALL TONGUE OF WOOD
LEFT BETWEEN LINKS,
REMOVED USING A DRILL
OR BURR IN A SMALL
ELECTRIC HAND HELD DRILL.

FIG. 6

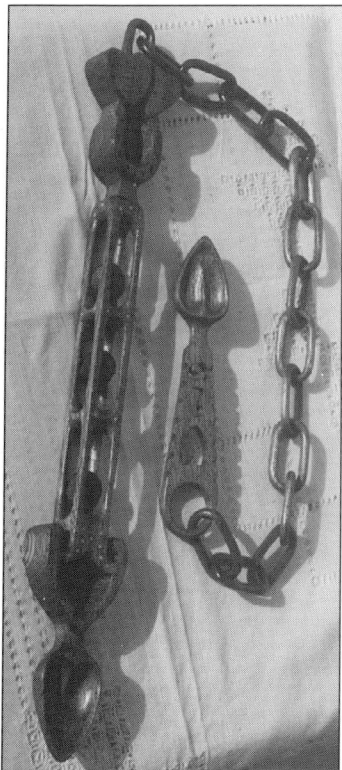

Our family spoon.

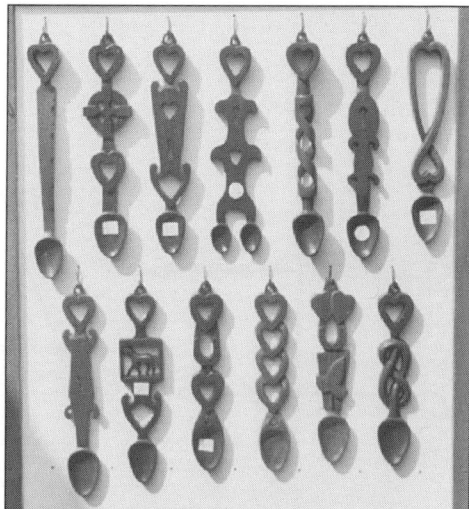

A few simple spoon shapes that I have made.

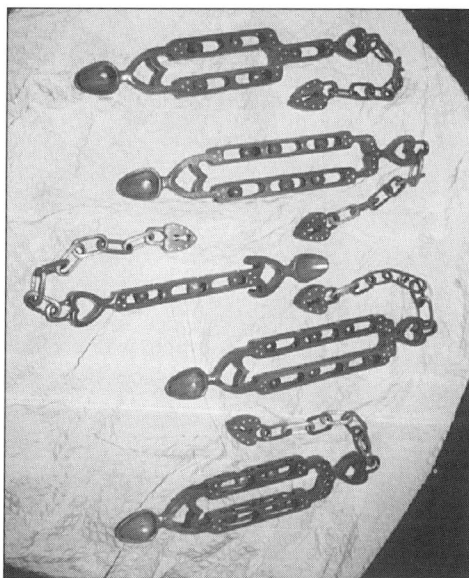

Multi-ball spoons made for an American family with five daughters. Each ball represents the number of children each daughter has.

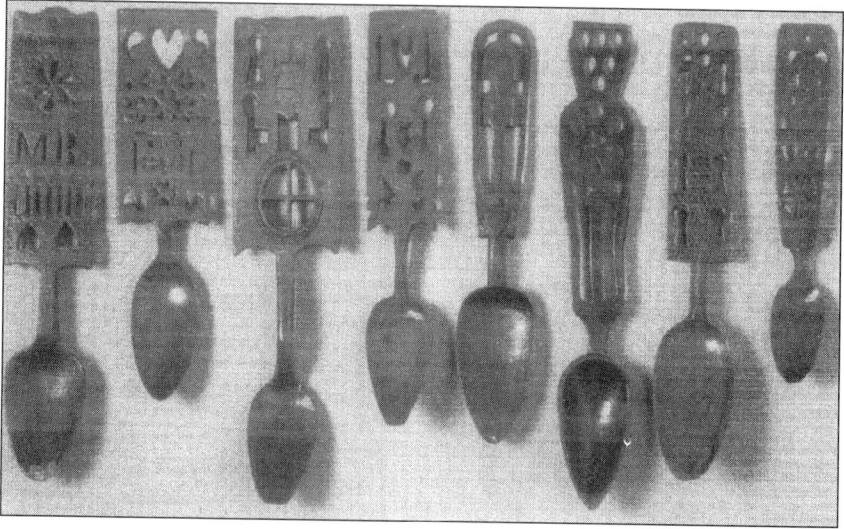

342   349   351   352   350   351   352   348

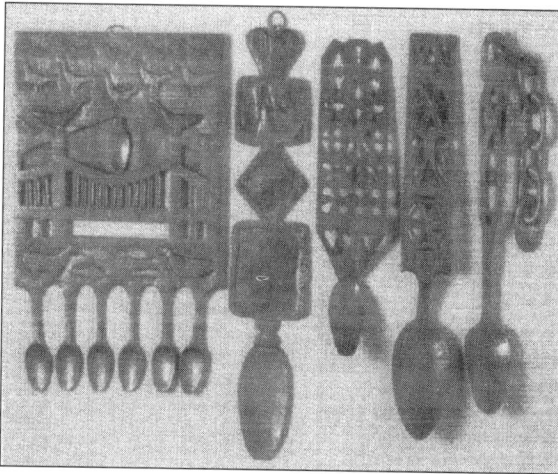

343   347   345 346 344

These 19th Century love spoons were sold at Sothebys on the 29 Feb. 2000.
The prices the spoons fetched were as follows:
342: £572; 349: £580; 351: £800; 352 (2 spoons): £650;
350: £580; 351: £800; 348: £1,495; 343: £3,600; 347: £287; 345: £1,500;
346: £552; 344: £1,092.

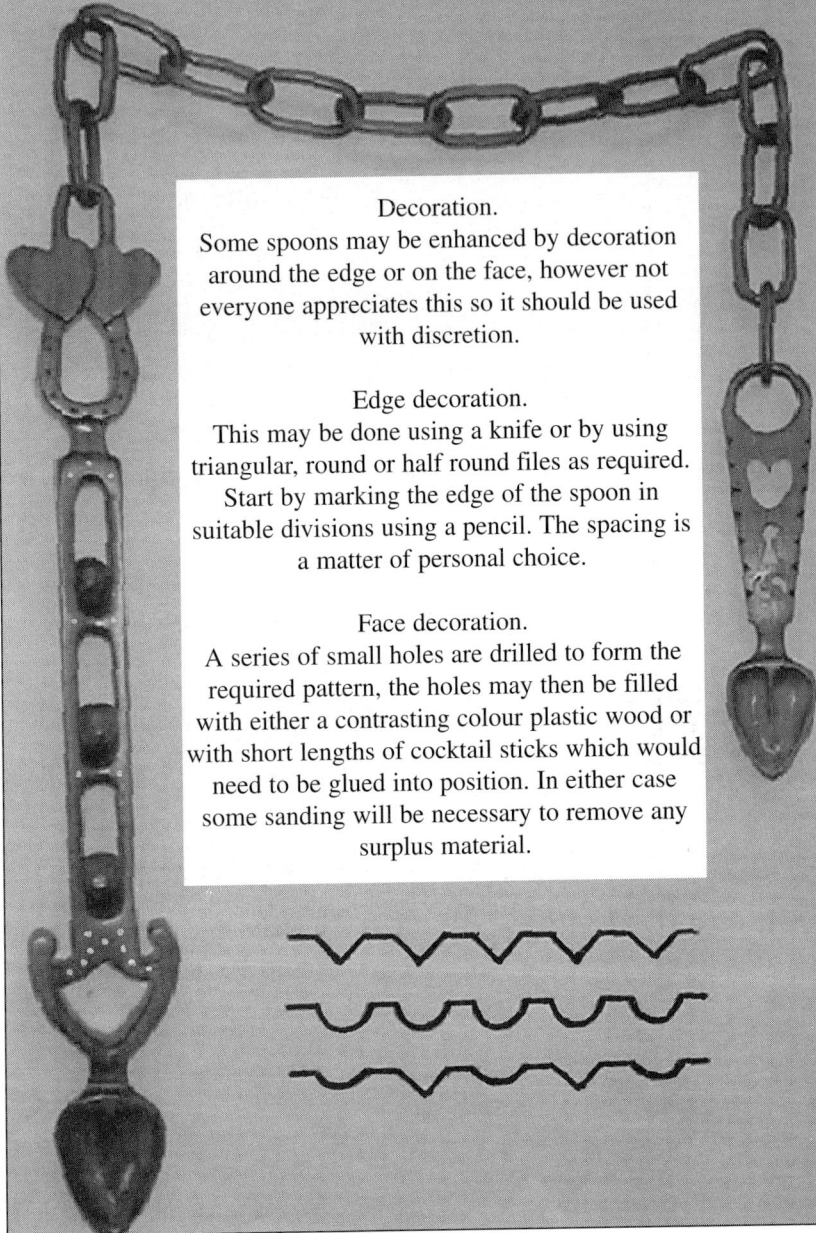

Decoration.

Some spoons may be enhanced by decoration around the edge or on the face, however not everyone appreciates this so it should be used with discretion.

Edge decoration.

This may be done using a knife or by using triangular, round or half round files as required. Start by marking the edge of the spoon in suitable divisions using a pencil. The spacing is a matter of personal choice.

Face decoration.

A series of small holes are drilled to form the required pattern, the holes may then be filled with either a contrasting colour plastic wood or with short lengths of cocktail sticks which would need to be glued into position. In either case some sanding will be necessary to remove any surplus material.

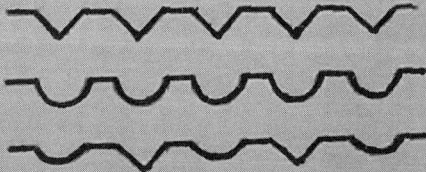

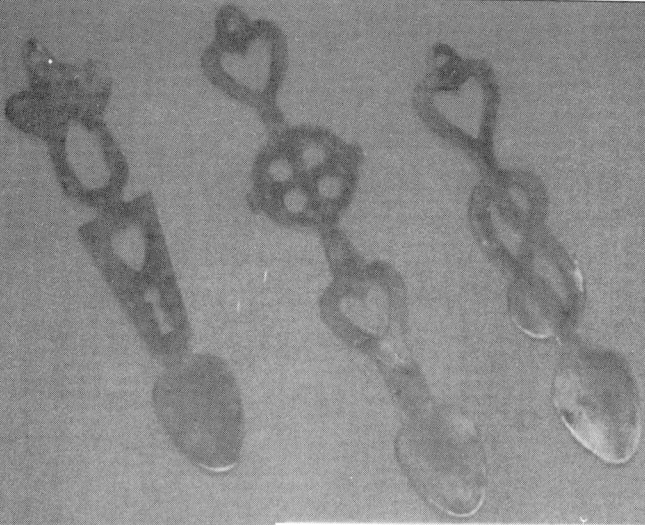

Aluminium templates for spoons which are frequently produced.

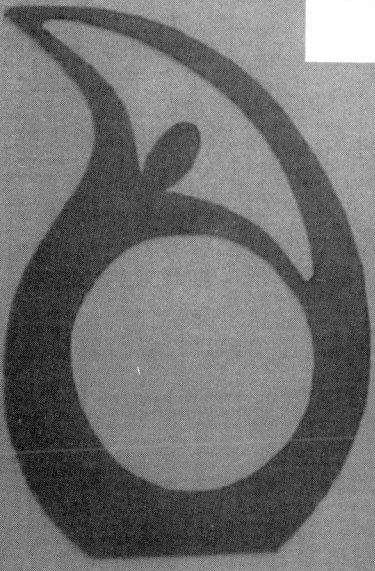

A cardboard template, used occasionally when marking-out Circular Dancing Girl.

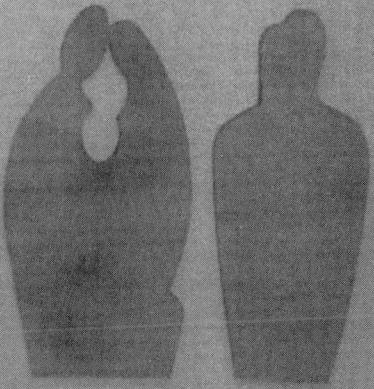

Plywood template for the Lovers. More durable than cardboard but may be easier to make than metal ones.

15 cm. Produce a sketch on a piece of paper like the one shown in Fig. 7 drawn to these dimensions. Cut this out and wrap it around your cylinder, the edges should match up, secure with an elastic band. Using a bradawl, pierce through the paper at numerous points along the line, remove the paper and join up the points using a Biro. Place the shank of the spoon in a vee block, held in the vice, then using a round file carefully follow the line you have drawn, when the desired depth has been reached turn the spoon over and file the other groove. Fig. 8. If the grooves are to go right through, filing would be very laborious. So instead of filing, a series of overlapping holes are drilled working from both sides of the stem, these should meet in the centre of the stem if the marking out has been accurately done. The holes must now be linked together using a knife. A round or half round file may then be used to remove much of the surplus wood followed by the inevitable sanding.

Now that you have the basic information it is just a matter of practice. The number of different designs you can create is infinite, just allow your imagination to go into overdrive.

Carving Bowls

Spoons were the starting point of my carving hobby but as time went by I felt the need to try something different so my next venture was to design and carve wooden bowls. Turned bowls are essentially circular in shape due to the method used to produce them. Carved bowls take longer to produce but they can be made in a large variety of shapes.

A simple shape to start with is an oval or elliptical bowl. The proportion of length to breadth is important, if the bowl is too long and narrow or too squat in shape it may not have the same aesthetic appeal as one of better proportions. A ratio known as the Golden Section has long been used in art and architecture to give a proportion which is pleasing to the eye of most people. Having said this there are times when it may be desirable to deviate widely from this ratio but it does form a good starting

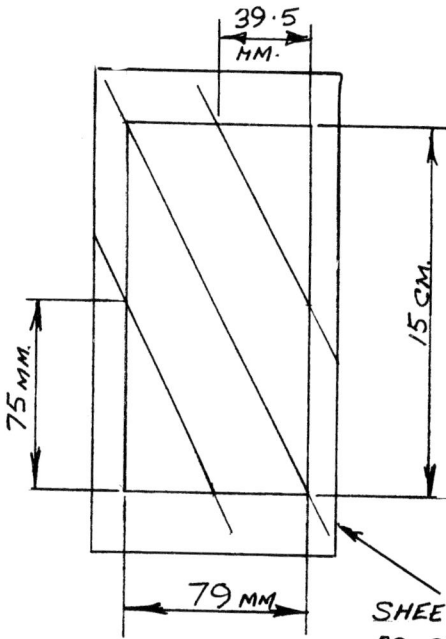

FIG. 7

SHEET OF PAPER MARKED OUT
AS SHOWN PRODUCES A
SPIRAL WHEN WRAPPED
AROUND A 25mm. DIA.
CYLINDER.

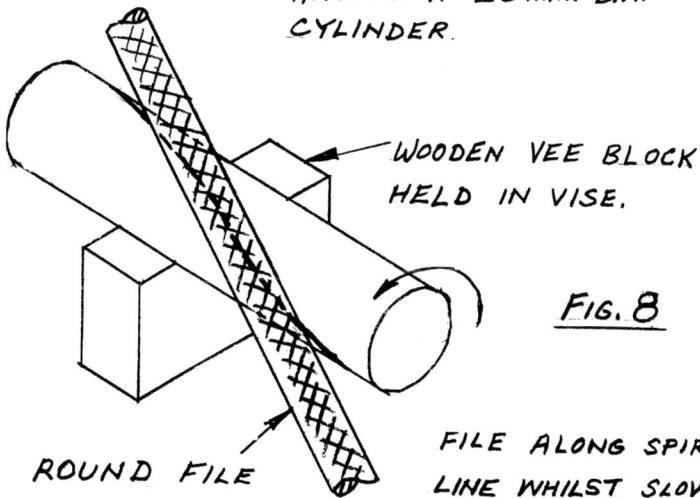

WOODEN VEE BLOCK
HELD IN VISE.

FIG. 8

ROUND FILE

FILE ALONG SPIRAL
LINE WHILST SLOWLY
ROTATING WORK.

point. A rough approximation is 5:8 so a bowl 15cm. wide would have a length of 24cm.

Elliptical shapes can be constructed in a number of ways. The method I normally use is shown in Fig 9. On the piece of wood you have selected for your bowl draw in the centre lines AC & DE. Around these construct a rectangle the dimensions of which are the outside size of the bowl. Divide AB into 4 equal parts and the line AF into the same number of parts. From point D draw lines through points 1, 2, & 3 on line AB and from point E draw lines to points 4, 5, & 6 on line AF. Where the lines intersect are points on the ellipse. Repeat the construction in the other three rectangles. Join the points together freehand or use a French curve. If this line represents the outside of the bowl, another line must be drawn 8 to 10mm. inside the first line to represent the inside edge of the bowl.

Having marked out the bowl profile on the wood it is usually easier to hollow out the bowl first. This can be done using a gouge. I find it easier if I remove some of the surplus wood from the centre of the bowl using a drill, but if this is done care must be taken not to drill too deeply at any point as the wood once removed cannot easily be replaced without it being apparent.

Once the bowl has been roughed out to the required shape using the gouge, it can be brought to a reasonable finish using a flap wheel in a hand held electric drill, this must inevitably be followed by hand sanding to remove any remaining ridges.

The outside of the bowl is easier to shape, first cut out the profile of the bowl using a band saw if available, additional wood may be removed by setting the bandsaw table to an angle of 45 degrees. Surform tools are a very useful way to quickly produce the required outside shape this can be followed using a spokeshave, file and sandpaper. Fig. 10.

Another shape, similar to the ellipses which can be easily constructed using large compasses or trammels is shown in Fig. 11. Start by drawing in centre lines on the piece of wood to be used for making the bowl. On these centre lines mark out the width and length of the bowl. It will be necessary to lay the work

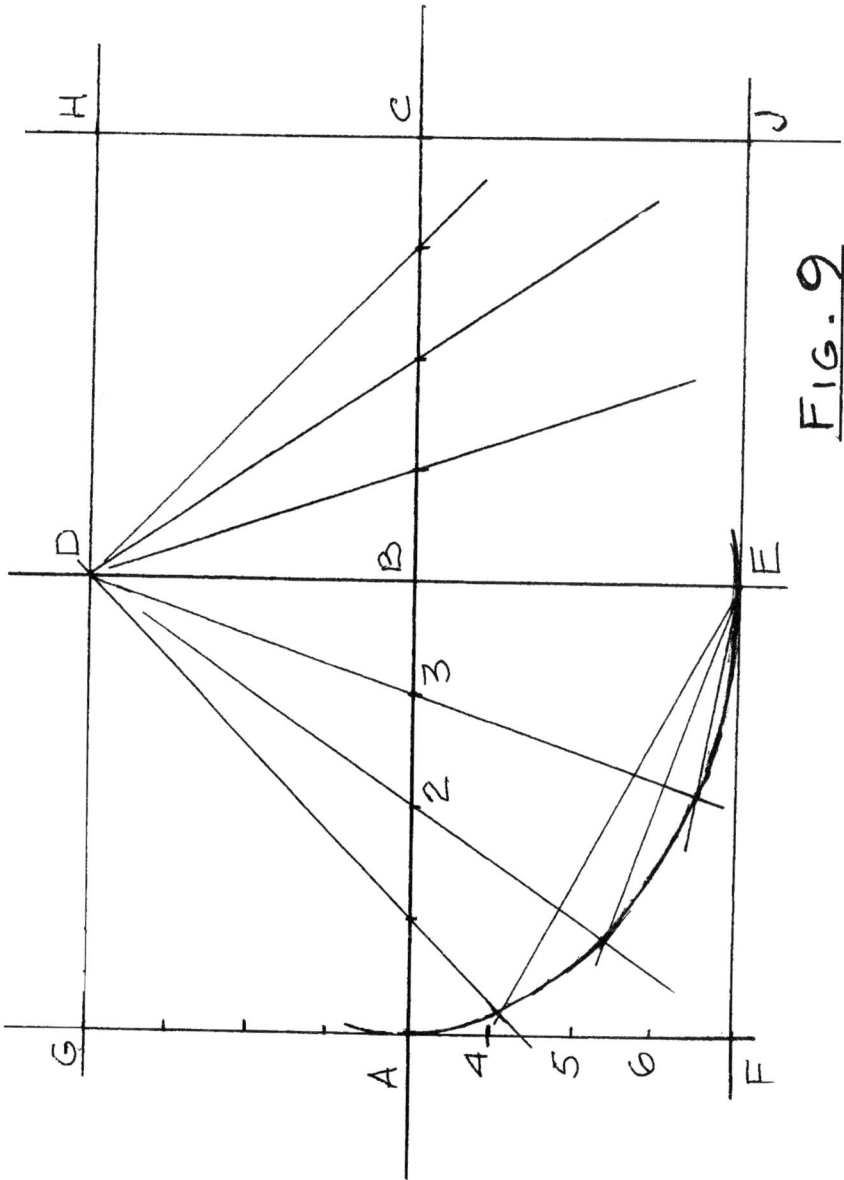

Fig. 9

23

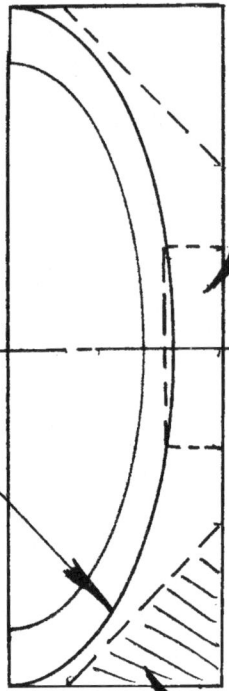

OUTSIDE PROFILE OF BOWL.

FIG.10

REMOVE SOME SURPLUS WOOD BY USING TILTING TABLE ON BAND SAW.

BASE MAY BE MADE INTEGRAL OR MAY BE MADE SEPARATELY AND GLUED TO BOWL.

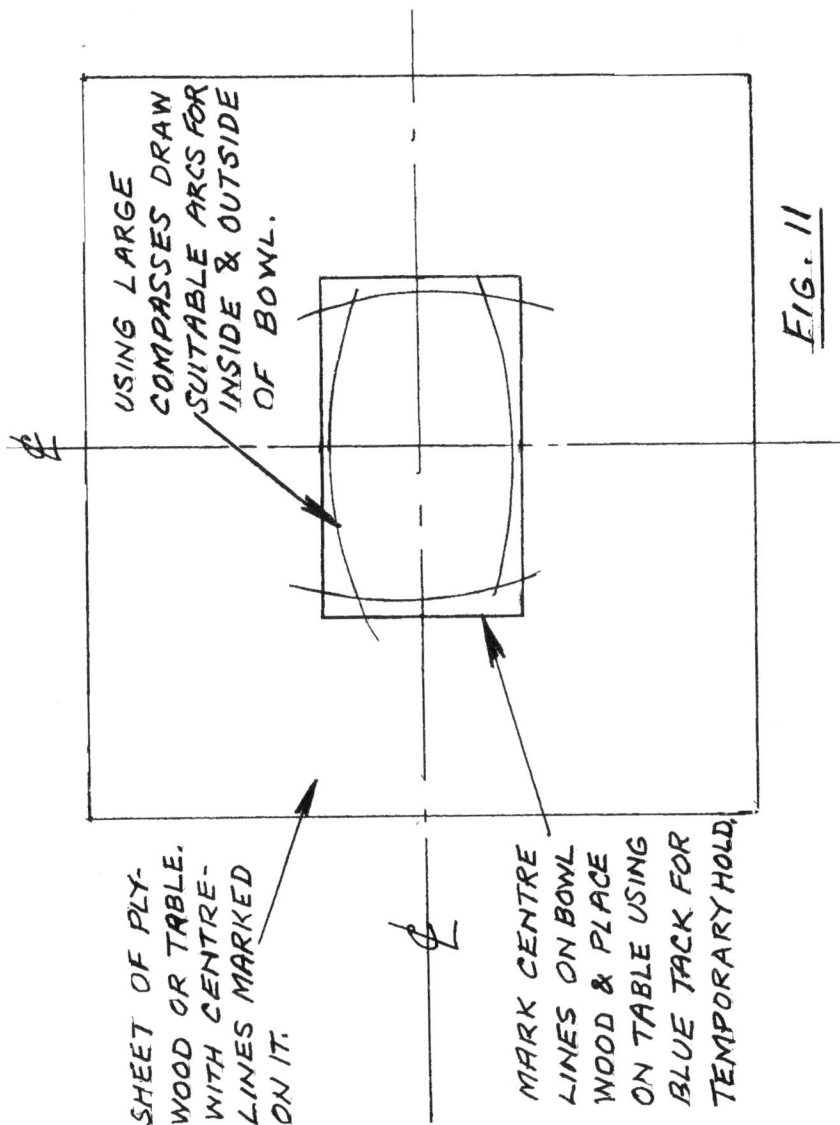

USING LARGE
COMPASSES DRAW
SUITABLE ARCS FOR
INSIDE & OUTSIDE
OF BOWL.

SHEET OF PLY-
WOOD OR TABLE.
WITH CENTRE-
LINES MARKED
ON IT.

MARK CENTRE
LINES ON BOWL
WOOD & PLACE
ON TABLE USING
BLUE TACK FOR
TEMPORARY HOLD.

FIG. 11

NAIL FILED TO SHARP
POINT & HAMMERED
THROUGH WOOD.

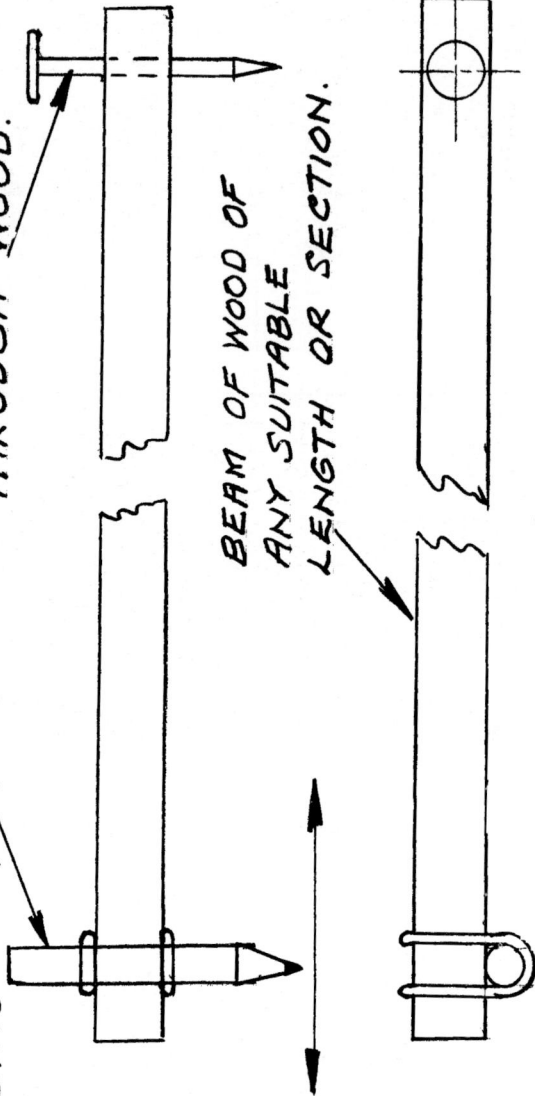

BEAM OF WOOD OF
ANY SUITABLE
LENGTH OR SECTION.

STRONG ELASTIC
BAND SECURING
BIRO OR PENCIL.

FIG. 12

26

Fig leaf bowl.

Assorted Yew bowls.

Ivy leaf bowl.

Circular fluted bowls.

Oval and fluted bowls.

An oval bowl with flutes.

on a large sheet of plywood or work table on which are drawn similar centrelines with which the work can be lined up. It is a matter of trial and error to find suitable radii for your particular design. The resulting shape can be quite pleasing.

A simple pair of trammels for marking out can be made by driving a nail through one end of a suitable length of wood and using an elastic band securing a pencil or Biro where required. Fig 12. It is advisable to secure the workpiece to the table temporarily using small pieces of blue tack or double sided tape.

Leaf shapes also make attractive bowls, fig leaves, ivy leaves or just plain apple leaves all make suitable shapes, the stem can be enlarged to provide a handle which makes the bowl suitable for bread, fruit or sweets which can be easily handed around.

Other bowls can be made with scalloped edges and flutes. Examples of some of the bowls I have made are shown in the various illustrations.

One other design feature to consider when making a bowl is the base, should this be an integral part of the bowl or should it be an addition? If the base is to be an integral part of the design considerably more work will be involved removing the surplus wood and of course the thickness of the initial piece of wood would have to take this into account. It is sometimes easier to cut out a circular or elliptical disc of the same sort of wood which can be glued to the underside of the bowl. If this option is chosen great care must be taken so that both the bowl and the base are absolutely flat so that the joint is invisible after gluing. The third option is to make feet, personally I prefer to make my feet dome shaped and always use three for stability. In some cases it may not be necessary to provide a plinth or feet.

The choice of timber used to make bowls is more important than for making spoons because of the much larger visible area. If you have a local timber merchant who deals with hard woods ask him if he has any offcuts available, most of the wood that I purchase has been obtained in this way at a fraction of the cost of similar pieces cut from a plank. When buying any timber examine it carefully to make sure that it has no cracks or splits, it can be very frustrating if you have carried out some of the work only to find that your time has been wasted.

Abstract Sculptures

These are essentially a figment of your imagination, the idea may be sparked off in a number of different ways, you may have a piece of wood containing knots or having an interesting grain pattern or it may be part of a branch of a tree suggesting a particular shape. Perhaps the best way to start the design process is with a good sized sheet of paper on which to sketch your preliminary idea, this will no doubt spark off other ideas which should also be sketched and so the creative process goes on gradually evolving and refining until you have produced something which looks promising. Never be satisfied with first thoughts, they will seldom produce the best results.

The next stage is to draw your design out accurately, full size if possible, from different angles so that you can see exactly what it should look like and will be able to assess how you will be able to make it. We all have a pretty good idea of our own limitations at any particular time and we have to limit our designs to suit our ability, the tools we have available and maybe the timber at our disposal. Having said that we should always strive for things which are just out of reach otherwise we don't make any progress. Personally I only started working with wood when I retired and have had no tuition using this material but I have an engineering background and am well acquainted with manufacturing processes.

Interlocking Forms started life as a fairly large piece of tree trunk from which I hoped to carve a head. When I had completed some of the preliminary work I noticed a crack developing, I left the work for a few days and the crack spread further so I decided not to proceed as it would probably ruin what would have been several weeks work, instead I split the trunk thinking I might be able to use one or both pieces for some other project, in the event after further cutting and shaping I ended up with Interlocking Forms and I was highly delighted when it was purchased by a quite well known sculptor.

Teardrop was made from a slab of elm which had been cut from a large elm tree which had died as a result of Dutch elm disease. Elm is quite a nice wood to work with and the grain of the timber is one of the best.

Whilst on holiday in Yorkshire I visited an exhibition of woodcarvings, one item intrigued me and when we returned home I tried to reproduce it on paper, this was quite unsuccessful so I decided to make a small three dimensional model. I was then able to make a full size carving working from this. It was an excellent exercise in three dimensional work. I have since made a second carving of the same design but from a different wood. I followed this by another more complex carving, each of these is called Everlasting.

The name derived partly from the fact that the carving has no beginning and no end and partly because they each took so long to make. I don't always work on one job from start to finish, in fact the carving of Everlasting 3 was spread over several months and I often wondered if it would ever be finished. It is the most difficult thing that I have ever made and it is one of the few carvings that I would be reluctant to part with.

Wherever we go I am always on the lookout for anything that might give me inspiration for something new, I'm always attracted by anything which has nice smooth curves and looking in the window of a china shop one day I saw what I thought was a beautiful ceramic figure of a dancing lady. Being made of china it contained a lot of detail and colour, when I decided to make a carving, based on the original, I had to simplify the design to make it suitable for carving, the head for example was in great detail which I would be unable to carve so I replaced this with the elliptical shape that you can see. On a number of other carvings that I have made I have done the same thing.

Ym-Yang is an old Chinese proverb which says that there is some good in the worst of us and some bad in the best. This is often displayed in the form of a circle divided into two comma

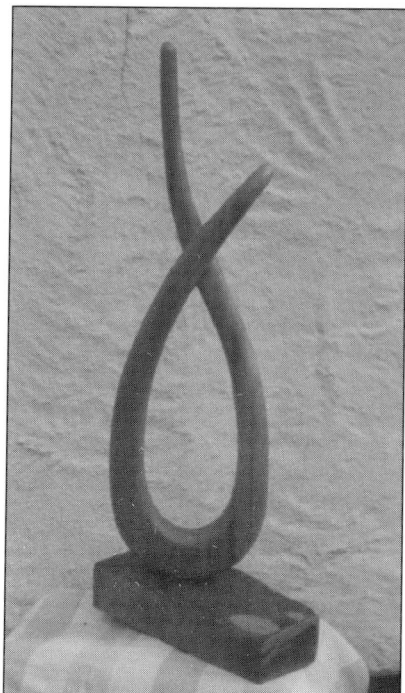
Teardrop.

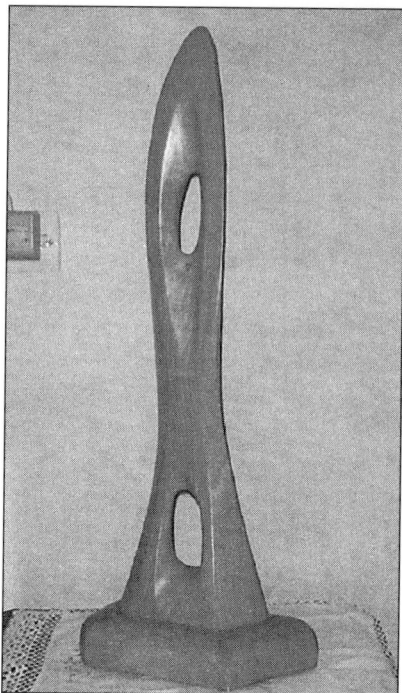
Two hole monolith.

Interlocking forms.

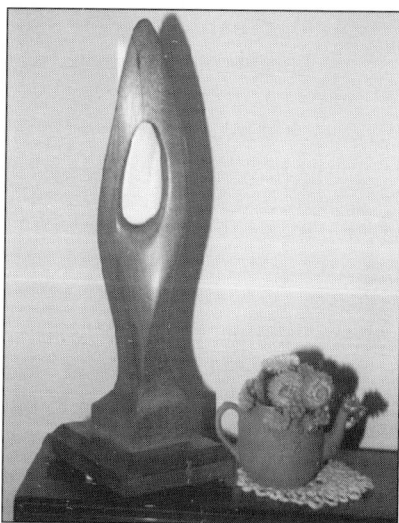
One hole monolith.

Everlasting 1.

Everlasting 2.

Everlasting 3.

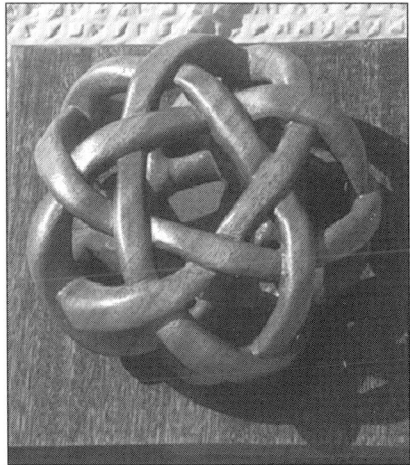

Everlasting 4.

shaped parts one black and the other white, in the centre of the black area is a white spot and in the centre of the white area is a black spot. I used this idea for my three dimensional Yin-Yang.

Most abstract work is very personal and may not be to everyones taste but this should not stop you from developing an idea as sooner or later you will find someone who has similar tastes to your own.

Using Stems and Branches of Trees

Small pieces of log and even branches of a tree or shrub can sometimes be used to make something interesting the most important thing about using wood of this sort is that it is often unseasoned in which case it might be a year or two before it can be used without it splitting or cracking.

A friend of mine once gave me some small branches of a yew tree, I decided that I would use these to make some ornamental goblets, in the stems of two of these I made captive balls like the ones described previously, a third, which was cut from a Y junction between two branches, was carved into a double goblet with a twisted stem.

Whilst walking along the shore one day I came across a small shrub, I took it home thinking that it might have some potential if I could only think what. It lay untouched for quite a while then I trimmed off some of the branches and roots and turned it upside down as shown on page 36. This then revealed arms legs and torso but unfortunately no head. I cleaned off the bark and by slimming down the branches was able to improve their shape a little. Using wood of this sort we are very much restricted in what we can do because we only have a limited amount of surplus material to play with. The head had to be carved and attached to the body, the joint being covered by a narrow green garland. The finished figure was mounted on a piece of yew and given the title of Woodland Nymph.

A similar chain of events resulted in the creation of the Welsh Dragon. Our garden sported a weeping cherry tree which had to

The dancers.

Hall chair to complement carvings
on grandfather clock.

Goblets made from small yew logs.

Rough tree partly trimmed.

Further trimming reveals possibilities.

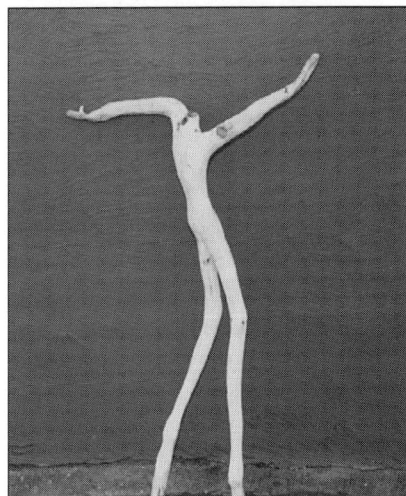
Bark and surplus roots removed.

Head added and final shaping
completed for Woodland Nymph.

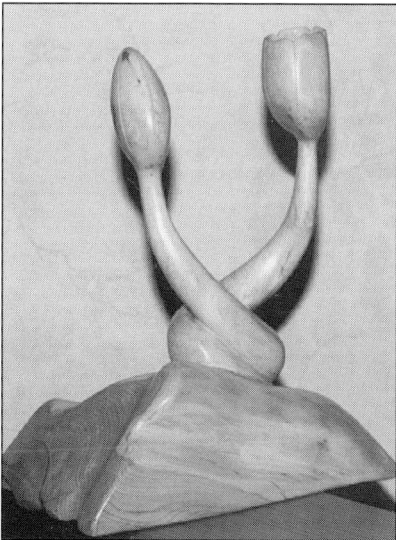

Examples of carvings made from branches of trees.

be removed. Page 39 shows the tree after the removal of some of the surplus branches and the completed dragon before painting. The head was carved and then attached to the body, the feet were also additional and were provided with claws made from old ebony piano keys. The wings were made from plywood with plywood ribs. The body was wrapped with an onion bag which was then coated with fibre glass resin which when painted gave a scaly effect. What does a real Welsh Dragon look like anyway?

Another small log was used to carve the dancing couple. The heads are featureless as I find great difficulty in carving faces. The finished work was sprayed with metallic paint to give it a bronze effect.

Odds and ends

I like to try my hand at a variety of work. This may not result in producing work of a high standard but it does add to the interest. Once again we were on holiday and this time in Germany when we visited Cologne cathedral. On looking around I was struck by the very fine carvings on the ends of the pews, they were so interesting that I decided to photograph them. When the prints arrived I thought that with some modification it would make a carved wall hanging. Some time before I had bought some small oak panels about 10mm. thick. They were badly warped into a gentle curve but I thought that this might add to the finished effect and so did not attempt to flatten them. I used two panels, one for the pierced work and the other for the backing. The wood was finished smooth with sand paper and then the design was drawn on the surface. Holes were drilled wherever possible and a coping saw used to remove the surplus wood. Edges and corners can be tidied up using small files. The carving of the flowers, leaves and stems can now take place. The veining on the leaves can be carried out using a vee edged disc wheel in a small hand held electric drill or using a knife, the stamens in the flowers consist of small holes grouped close together, using a bradawl or similar tool. I placed a piece of

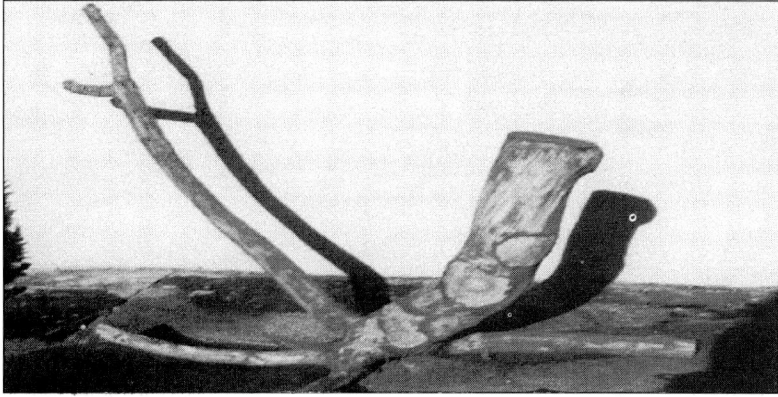

Stages in the production of the Welsh dragon.

Carvings on pew ends in Cologne
Cathedral.

Wall plaque based on carvings on
pew ends.

green material between the front and back panels to give the carving greater effect. If I were to make another similar carving I would undercut the leaves and stems to give a more realistic effect. Whilst the quality of the carving is not to be compared with that of the original it gave me a great deal of pleasure in making it.

Still Life in the Garden Shed was another one-off effort, it was a picture built up in low relief using separate pieces of wood for each item. The back of the shed and floor was made by gluing thin strips of wood to a plywood base, panel pins were used to simulate nails. The contents of the shed were then made individually and glued into place. The overall effect was reasonably three dimensional and when shown in a local exhibition received some favourable comments before being purchased.

Furniture making requires a great deal of skill and many years of training. The only piece of furniture that I have ever attempted is a hall chair which I was persuaded to make to complement a 300 year old carved dark oak grandfather clock. I acquired some planks of oak in exchange for a Welsh love spoon. I had seen a chair of suitable design in one of the woodworking magazines and used this for the basic construction and design. The carving on the back of the chair was similar to that on the carcass of the clock and that on the seat was copied from an illustration.

The finished chair was stained to match the clock and although not the most comfortable seat in the house it does complement the clock. All the carving is fairly low relief and the background is finished with a matting tool.

In another illustration you will see a group of people sitting on a settee, this is The Wood Family, each member of the family is made from a different sort of wood, as in some other pieces all of the family are featureless.

From the illustrations that follow you can see that I have attempted to produce a variety of carvings, some with more success than others. Whatever the result, something was learnt

Two ball sculpture.

Goblet with ball in stem.

One ball sculpture.

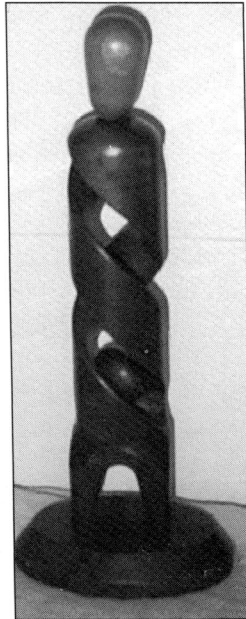

Woman
with
Child. Ball
in twisted
stem.

The lovers.

Kneeling lady.

Dancing girl.

Praying hands.

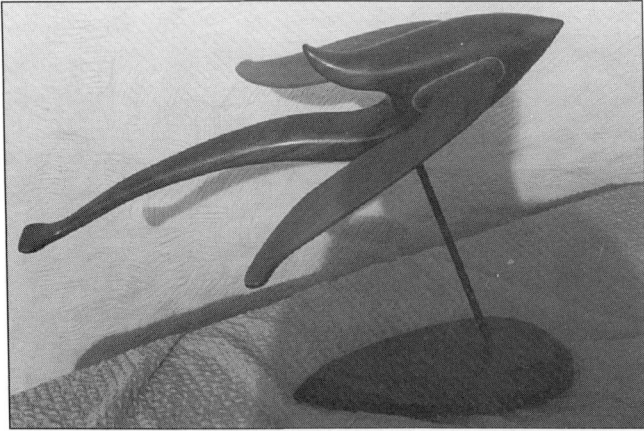

Flight.

Friendship.

Father time.

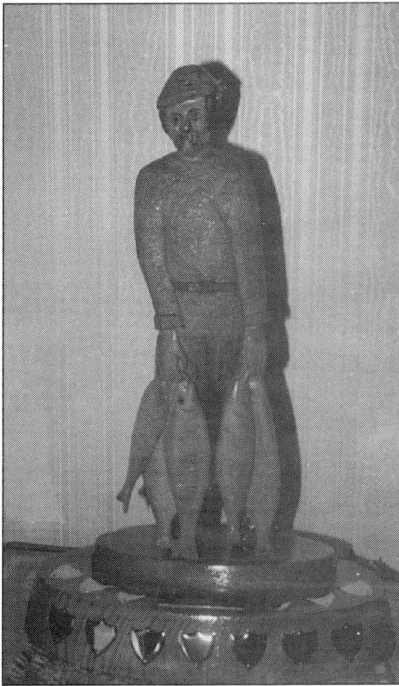

Fishing club trophy.

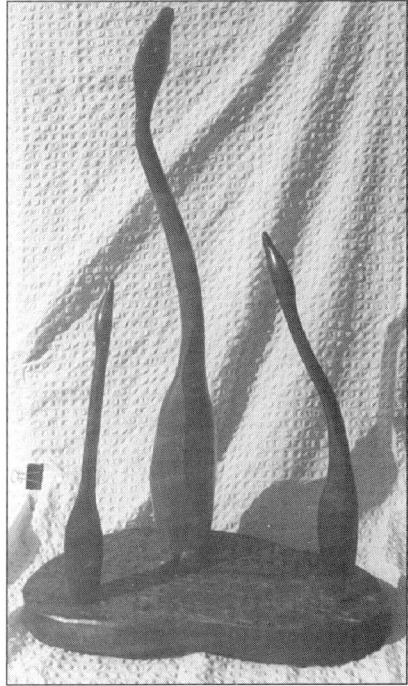

Goose talk.

The
thinkers.

Leaf carving.

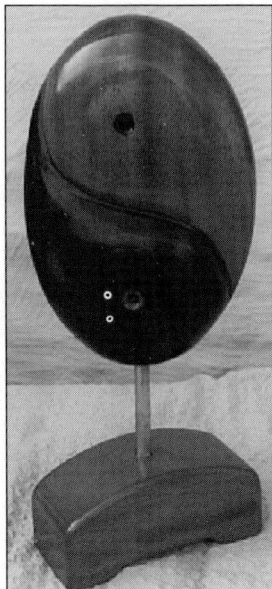
Yin Yang.

Carving based on a particular species of seaweed.

Above: Each item carved in low relief and then glued to the base.
Left: Leaping salmon.
Below: Each item in this carving is made from a different sort of wood.

during its production. Perhaps limiting my scope would have improved my workmanship, on the other hand variety is said to be the spice of life. It has certainly done much to maintain my enthusiasm for the hobby.

Pricing your work

If you take up carving seriously as a hobby you will soon saturate your friends and family with your work and like me, will have to find other outlets.

Gift and craft shops are often eager to sell your work but beware, most will take 30% commission and often work on the basis of sale or return. If you should sell work in this way make sure that you and they keep accurate records of any transactions.

A craftworkers organisation is often a better proposition as they invariably organise craft fairs at which each individual has a stall. This can be fun you meet other craftworkers and of course potential customers.

Spoons are easy to price as you can compare yours with those on sale in craft shops and price yours accordingly. Other items may be more difficult to price but if you have a rough idea about how many hours it has taken you to produce the work and multiply this by your assumed hourly wage plus the cost of materials, overheads etc. you will probably reach an astronomical figure which would mean that you would sell little and would accumulate a pile of expensive firewood. We have to be realistic and realise that it is only the expert who can charge what he likes. If your work is unique and has aesthetic or artistic merit this will of course influence the selling price, its often a case of testing the market to establish a suitable starting point.